# MOUNTAIN FOOD CHAINS

Rachel Lynette

**www.raintreepublishers.co.uk**
Visit our website to find out
more information about
Raintree books.

**To order:**
☎ Phone 0845 6044371
🖩 Fax +44 (0) 1865 312263
✉ Email myorders@raintreepublishers.co.uk

Customers from outside the UK please telephone +44 1865 312262

Raintree is an imprint of Capstone Global Library Limited,
a company incorporated in England and Wales having its
registered office at 7 Pilgrim Street, London, EC4V 6LB
– Registered company number: 6695582

Text © Capstone Global Library Limited 2011
First published in hardback in 2011
The moral rights of the proprietor have been asserted.

Edited by Abby Colich and Andrew Farrow
Designed by Victoria Allen
Illustrated by Words and Publications
Picture research by Mica Brancic
Originated by Capstone Global Library Ltd
Printed by China Translation & Printing Services Ltd

ISBN 978 0 431 01381 7 (hardback)
14 13 12 11 10
10 9 8 7 6 5 4 3 2 1

**British Library Cataloguing in Publication Data**
Lynette, Rachel.
Mountain food chains. -- (Protecting food chains)
577.5'316-dc22
A full catalogue record for this book is available from the
British Library.

**Acknowledgments**
The author and publisher are grateful to the following for
permission to reproduce copyright material: Alamy p. **41**
(© Tom Uhlman); Dr Sylvain Dubey p. **28** (School of
Biological Sciences, The University of Sydney); Getty
Images p. **43** (Jessica Peterson); iStockphoto p. **42** (© Loretta
Hostettler); Photolibrary pp. **4** (Robert Harding Travel/James
Hager), **9** (Picture Press/Peter Weimann), **13** (The Irish
Image Collection), **14** (age fotostock/Werner Bollmann),
**15** (age fotostock/Loren Irving), **17** (All Canada Photos/
John E. Marriott), **18** (age fotostock/Mark Jones), **19** (age
fotostock/Eric Baccega), **21**, **22** (Oxford Scientific (OSF)/
Daniel J. Cox), **23** (Picture Press/Helge Schulz), **26** (Phototake
Science/Dennis Kunkel), **27** (F1 Online/Schulz Schulz),
**31** (Juniors Bildarchiv), **33** (Oxford Scientific (OSF)/Tom
Ulrich), **34** (White), **35** (Aurora Photos/Harrison Shull), **36**
(Oxford Scientific (OSF)/Mary Plage), **37** (Oxford Scientific
(OSF)/Richard Packwood), **38** (imagebroker.net/Gerhard
Zwerger-Schoner), **39** (All Canada Photos/Keith Douglas), **40**
(agefotostock/Werner Bollmann); Shutterstock pp. **8** (© Vaclav
Volrab); **25** (© D. & K. Kucharscy).

Cover photograph of a mountain lion (Felis concolor) chasing
prey in snow, Minnesota, reproduced with permission of
Photolibrary (age fotostock/Ronald Wittek).

Cover and spread background image reproduced with
permission of Shutterstock (© Elisabeth Holm and © WizData
Inc.).

We would like to thank Kenneth Dunton and Dana Sjostrom
for their invaluable help in the preparation of this book.

Every effort has been made to contact copyright holders of any
material reproduced in this book. Any omissions will
be rectified in subsequent printings if notice is given to
the publisher.

**Disclaimer**
All the internet addresses (URLs) given in this book were valid
at the time of going to press. However, due to the dynamic
nature of the internet, some addresses may have changed, or
sites may have changed or ceased to exist since publication.
While the author and publisher regret any inconvenience this
may cause readers, no responsibility for any such changes can
be accepted by either the author or the publisher.

# CONTENTS

Words appearing in bold, **like this**, are explained in the glossary.

# WHAT IS A MOUNTAIN FOOD CHAIN?

Have you ever gone walking in the mountains? If so, you probably saw many different plants and animals. The plants and animals on a mountain all depend on one another for survival.

All the animals that live on a mountain must eat plants or other animals to survive. Blue sheep, for example, **graze** on grass growing in meadows in the Himalaya Mountains in Central Asia. Blue sheep are sometimes eaten by snow leopards. When a snow leopard dies, **bacteria** break down the remains into **nutrients**. Some of the nutrients go back into the soil, where they help plants grow. Then the process can begin again. This process is called a food chain.

These mountain goats get energy from the grass they eat.

## ALL ABOUT ENERGY

All **organisms** need **energy**. A food chain shows how energy moves from one organism to another. The arrows show how energy moves up the food chain. When a plant or animal is eaten by another animal, most of its energy is lost. Some of its energy transfers to the animal that eats it. For example, grass gives energy to blue sheep. Blue sheep give energy to snow leopards, and so on.

## PROTECTING FOOD CHAINS

Humans have caused a great deal of damage to mountain food chains. Mountain food chains are often more fragile than food chains in other parts of the world. This is because very few plants and animals can survive high up on a mountain. We need to protect mountain **habitats** so that all organisms can grow and thrive.

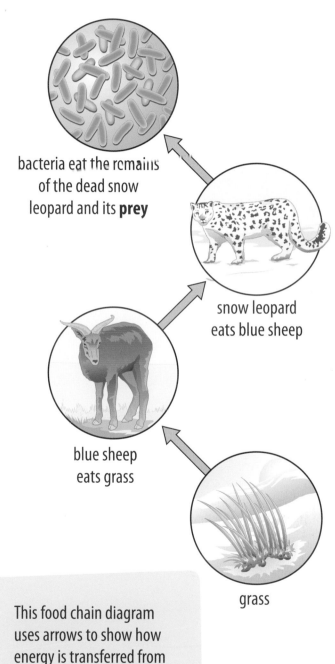

bacteria eat the remains of the dead snow leopard and its **prey**

snow leopard eats blue sheep

blue sheep eats grass

grass

This food chain diagram uses arrows to show how energy is transferred from one organism to another.

# LINKS IN THE CHAIN

Plants get their energy from the Sun. Their leaves capture some of the Sun's energy. Then they use a process called **photosynthesis** to convert that energy from the Sun into food. Plants are the first link in all food chains. Because they make their own food, plants are called **producers**. They also produce food that other organisms eat.

Next in the chain are **primary consumers**. Primary consumers are animals that eat plants. **Herbivores** are animals that eat only plants. Herbivores are primary consumers.

Next in the chain are **secondary consumers**. They eat primary consumers or other secondary consumers. They might be **carnivores** or **omnivores**. Carnivores are animals that eat only other animals. Omnivores eat both plants and animals.

When a plant or animal dies, it may be eaten by **scavengers**. The scavengers leave behind matter that **decomposers** go to work on. Decomposers, such as bacteria and **fungi**, break down dead plant and animal matter into nutrients. The nutrients go back into the soil to help new plants grow. This allows food chain cycles to continue.

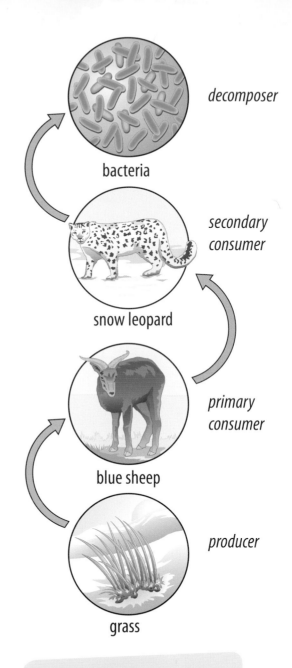

decomposer

bacteria

secondary consumer

snow leopard

primary consumer

blue sheep

producer

grass

This food chain shows how energy is passed from producer to **consumer** to decomposer.

# MOUNTAIN FOOD WEBS

Most animals in a mountain food chain eat several different organisms. If an animal depends on just one organism for food, it could die if that organism becomes scarce. Animals that eat many different kinds of food have a better chance of survival than those with more limited choices. Because they eat many different organisms, these animals are a part of many different food chains.

A food web is many food chains put together. The arrows in a food web show how energy moves from one organism to another. A small change in the web, such as the loss of one organism, can affect many different plants and animals.

This food web shows how mountain organisms depend on each other for food.

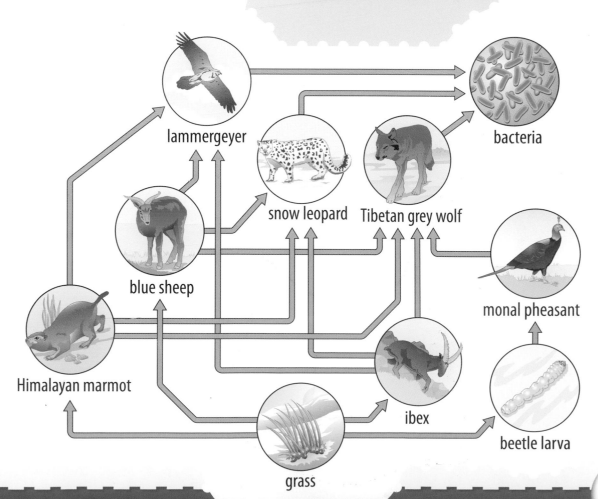

lammergeyer

bacteria

snow leopard

Tibetan grey wolf

blue sheep

monal pheasant

Himalayan marmot

ibex

beetle larva

grass

# WHAT IS A MOUNTAIN HABITAT?

Mountains are areas of land higher than hills. The highest mountains in the world are in the Himalaya Mountains in Asia. This includes the very highest mountain, Mount Everest.

The **summits** of many mountains are covered in snow all year long. Cold weather, wind, and snow make it difficult – or even impossible – for plants to grow. The **habitat** changes further down the mountain. As the weather gets warmer, more plants can grow. Mountain habitats also vary by location. Mount Kilimanjaro in Africa has different habitats from Mount McKinley in Alaska, for example.

This photo shows just some of the diversity of life in a mountain habitat.

# MOUNTAIN ADAPTATIONS

Plants and animals that live in mountain habitats have developed special features called **adaptations**. These adaptations help them survive in harsh environments. For example, yaks and mountain goats have thick coats of fur to keep them warm. Some mountain wildflowers even have hair to help keep them warm. The leaves and flowers of edelweisses are covered with tiny hairs that look like felt.

Other animals make it through the long, cold winter by **hibernating**, or resting for long periods of time. Bears, white-tailed prairie dogs, marmots, and ground squirrels all hibernate. Over the winter months, **mammals** use extra body fat to stay warm and avoid freezing. Some amphibians' and reptiles' bodies stay frozen all winter!

## ANIMAL ADAPTATIONS: STAY WARM OR BLEND IN?

Many **alpine** mammals have dark fur. Dark colours absorb sunlight and help the animal stay warm. Some animals, such as the snowshoe hare and Arctic fox, have fur that turns white to match the snow. These animals may not stay as warm as ones with dark fur, but they are safer from **predators.**

This Arctic fox's white fur helps it to blend in with the snow.

# WHERE IN THE WORLD ARE MOUNTAIN HABITATS?

This map shows some of the main mountains of the world.

Mt McKinley

The Alaskan Range

NORTH AMERICA

The Appalachian Mountains

Rocky Mountains

Mt Huascaran

SOUTH AMERICA

Andes Mountains

ASIA

The Caucasus
Mountains

EUROPE

The Pyrenees
The Alps

The Himalayas

▲ Mt Everest

The Atlas
Mountains

AFRICA

The Ethiopian
Highlands

▲ Mt Kenya
▲ Mt Kilimanjaro

AUSTRALIA

ANTARCTICA

# WHAT ARE THE PRODUCERS ON MOUNTAINS?

Different kinds of plant live at different **elevations** (heights) on a mountain. The plants near the **summit** are different from those near the base. Rainforests or broad-leaf trees grow at lower levels. **Conifers** grow at higher **altitudes**. Above a certain altitude, no trees can grow at all. This is called the **timberline**. Plants that grow between the timberline and the summit must **adapt** to a harsher **climate**. These plants include shrubs, wildflowers, and grasses. On some mountains, nothing grows at the summit, where there is snow all year long. On other mountains, there are small patches of soil where a few hardy plants grow.

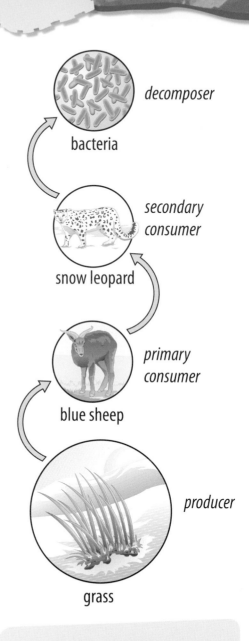

decomposer
bacteria

secondary consumer
snow leopard

primary consumer
blue sheep

producer
grass

## TWISTED TREES

Conifers that grow near the timberline may be affected by the climate. When the wind kills all the branches on one side of a tree, the tree has a flag shape. Other trees become stunted and twisted by the harsh weather. They might even grow sideways to stay closer to the ground. This is called a Krummholz formation.

Grass, a **producer**, gets its energy from the Sun. The energy is transferred when the grass is eaten by **consumers**.

The harsh mountain weather has caused this hawthorn tree to grow sideways.

## COLD WEATHER CONIFERS

Conifers such as pines, furs, and spruces are adapted to live in harsh mountain climates. The needles on a conifer are actually its leaves! The small, thin needles conserve (save) **energy** better than broad leaves. The needles' waxy coating helps to stop them from freezing during the harsh winter. Also, the needles on conifers do not fall off in the autumn (that is why they are called 'evergreens'). This means they can capture what little sunlight there is all year around.

The narrow shape of a conifer helps it shed snow. Conifers also have flexible branches that slope downwards. This helps the snow to slide off the branches, rather than weigh them down and break them.

## FLOWER POWER

Flowers, grasses, and shrubs can grow above the timberline. They have adapted to the harsh climate. Growing close to the ground helps keep them warm and out of the wind. Mountain wildflowers often have large, protective leaves. On many mountains, snow covers the ground for most of the year. Mountain flowers must be able to grow quickly once the snow melts in the spring. They produce flowers only during summer months. Some flowers can even grow through melting snow.

Bees, butterflies, and other **pollinators** are not as common high up on a mountain as they are lower down. Mountain wildflowers often have large, bright flowers. This helps them attract the few pollinators that can survive the harsh climate.

Growing in a hump helps these tiny moss campion flowers to survive.

### MOSS CAMPION

This hardy flower grows in the mountains of North America, the United Kingdom, and parts of Europe. The moss campion plant survives the harsh climate by growing in a rounded hump, or cushion. The cushion shape allows water to roll off. It also helps to keep the inner parts of the plant cushion warm, and protects the delicate buds from the weather. Several types of butterfly eat **nectar** from moss campion.

Lichen clings to this rock high on the mountain.

## LITTLE LICHENS

Lichens can thrive in high altitudes because they do not need soil to grow. Instead, they grow on rocks or other plants. Lichens are actually two **organisms** that live together in **symbiosis**. The outside of the lichen is a **fungus**, and the inside is an **alga**. The fungus provides protection for the alga. The alga provide food for the fungus through **photosynthesis**. Together they make up one of the hardiest organisms on the planet.

# WHAT ARE THE PRIMARY CONSUMERS ON MOUNTAINS?

Most **primary consumers** eat a wide variety of plants. But some eat just one. For example, the giant panda eats only bamboo. Plants are often scarce in the winter months, especially high up in the mountains. Many primary consumers **hibernate**, storing up food to get through the winter.

## IMPORTANT INSECTS

Insects that live high in the mountains must **adapt** to the wind and cold. Most of these insects do not have wings. If they could fly, they would just get blown away by the wind. Many mountain insects have hair to keep them warm and are dark in colour to absorb sunlight.

Insects eat a wide variety of plants. Several types of beetle eat tree bark. Insects with wings, such as bees, butterflies, and moths, **pollinate** wildflowers and other plants.

## RODENTS AND HARES

Many primary consumers are rodents that live underground. Marmots dig burrows where they hibernate during the winter. They eat grasses, berries, lichens, mosses, and wildflowers. When a group of marmots is eating, one acts as a guard. If the guard senses danger, it makes a loud whistling sound. Then all the marmots jump into their nearby burrows.

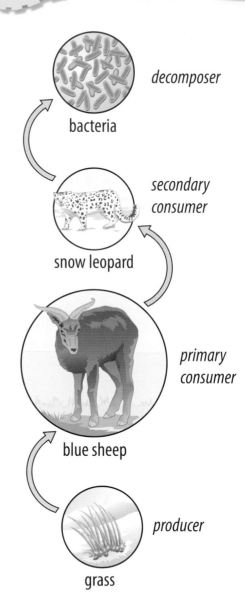

decomposer
bacteria

secondary
consumer
snow leopard

primary
consumer
blue sheep

producer
grass

Primary consumers, such as this blue sheep, eat plants.

Mountain pikas live in rock crevices and do not hibernate. Instead they collect grass and dry it to make hay for bedding. The hay keeps them warm all winter long. Sometimes a pika will steal another pika's hay.

## PROTECTING A LINK: VANCOUVER ISLAND MARMOT

The Vancouver Island marmot lives high in the mountains on Vancouver Island in Canada. **Climate change** and forest **clear-cutting** have caused their numbers to decline. Scientists believe that there are fewer than 100 left in the wild. They are Canada's most **endangered** animal.

Vancouver Island marmots' numbers have declined because of climate change and clear-cutting.

This vicuna keeps her baby safe by listening for predators.

## BIG GRAZERS

Large **grazing** animals often live in herds. The herd helps to keep individual animals warm. It also protects weaker animals from **predators**. Mountain goats live in North America. They have split hooves with soft pads for traction. The edges of their hooves can cut through ice. Mountain goats can climb steep, rocky slopes to heights their predators cannot reach. They spend most of their time grazing on grass, moss, ferns, and lichens.

Vicunas live in the Andes Mountains. They are related to alpacas and have thick, soft coats to keep them warm. They have good hearing to keep them safe from predators. Vicunas eat the tough grass that grows high in the mountains.

Wild yaks are found in the Himalaya Mountains. They have large lungs and hearts to adapt to air with less oxygen at higher **altitudes**. Thick coats also help to keep them warm. Yaks eat grass, lichen, small shrubs, and twigs.

## MOUNTAIN PRIMATES

Several **species** of **primate** (a group of animals that includes monkeys, apes, and humans) live in the mountains. Mountain gorillas live in Africa and eat more than 40 different kinds of plant. Snub-nosed monkeys live in the trees of the Himalaya Mountains. They eat fruit, leaves, bamboo buds, and tree needles. In the mountains of Japan, snow monkeys eat bark during the winter.

### LOSING A LINK: GIANT PANDAS

Giant pandas can be found in the wild on just a few mountains in central China. They are losing their **habitat** as people cut down the bamboo forests they live in. Giant pandas only eat bamboo, and they eat a lot of it. A single panda eats up to 14 kilograms (30 pounds) of bamboo each day!

Giant pandas spend most of their time feasting on bamboo.

# WHAT ARE THE SECONDARY CONSUMERS ON MOUNTAINS?

**Secondary consumers** depend on other animals for their food. Some secondary consumers hunt for food, while others are **scavengers**. Secondary consumers must save their **energy**. A **predator** that is weak from hunger may not be strong or fast enough to hunt.

## BIRDS OF PREY

Many birds **migrate** thousands of kilometres to feed on the insects that live in the mountains in the spring and summer. Larger birds, such as hawks and eagles, prey on small **mammals** such as rodents and hares. These birds have keen eyesight. They can spot **prey** from high in the air. They also have sharp beaks and **talons** for tearing flesh.

## WEASELS

Mountain weasels make nests in rock crevices. They eat mostly pika and voles. Wolverines are the largest members of the weasel family. A wolverine will attack another animal many times its own size. In addition to hunting, wolverines also eat dead animals.

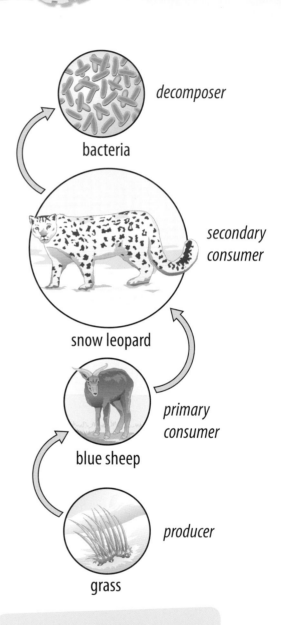

decomposer
bacteria

secondary consumer
snow leopard

primary consumer
blue sheep

producer
grass

Secondary consumers such as the snow leopard get energy by eating other animals.

A red fox chases a prairie dog.

## WILD DOGS

Several kinds of wild dog live in the mountains. Foxes eat whatever they can find – usually rodents such as pikas or mice. Foxes sometimes store extra food under a layer of snow. Coyotes hunt in pairs for small mammals such as hares and rodents. Wolves hunt in packs, often taking large grazing animals such as elk.

### PROTECTING A CHAIN: TOO MANY WOLVES?

In 2009, grey wolves were taken off the **endangered species** list in parts of the United States. This means people in some states can now hunt them. Some scientists are worried that killing the wolves will result in too many elk. Elk eat willow and aspen trees, which could become endangered if elk herds get too big.

## BIG CATS

Snow leopards can be found in Central and South Asia. They have several **adaptations** that help them to survive the cold **climate**. In addition to warm coats, snow leopards have long, bushy tails. They wrap their tails around themselves for extra warmth when they are sleeping. They also have larger lungs than other big cats. This helps them to breathe high on the mountain where there is not much oxygen. Snow leopards prey mostly on mountain sheep and goats but also eat smaller mammals.

In North and South America, cougars will eat anything they can catch, from insects to elks. Cougars have large paws that help them leap far while hunting for prey. Lynx live in the mountains of Europe, Asia, and North America. They eat both small and large mammals. They sometimes give their young live prey to play with before they kill and eat it.

A snow leopard has a thick coat to keep it warm.

This black bear eats both plants and animals.

## OMNIVORES

**Omnivores**, such as raccoons and bears, are both **primary** and secondary consumers. Raccoons are **native** to North America. They eat fruit, nuts, worms, and insects. Raccoons that live in the mountains sleep a lot during winter, when food is scarce. Their body functions slow down, and they wake up several times while **hibernating** during the winter.

Bears hibernate in the same way as raccoons, from October to April or May. In the spring and summer, they get most of their energy from berries, roots, and sprouts. They also eat insects, small mammals, fish, and occasionally large **grazing** animals.

### MOUNTAIN TIGERS

Even though most Bengal tigers do not live high in the mountains, some do. Photos have been taken of Bengals in the Himalayas at **altitudes** of up to about 4,000 metres (13,000 feet)!

# WHAT ARE THE DECOMPOSERS ON MOUNTAINS?

Scavengers and **decomposers** are important parts of the food chain. When a plant or animal dies, scavengers find and eat the remains. Decomposers then break down what the scavengers leave behind.

## MOUNTAIN SCAVENGERS

Some **carnivores** are also scavengers. If they cannot find an animal to kill, they may eat parts of a kill that another carnivore has left behind. Bears, coyotes, foxes, and birds such as vultures, eagles, and ravens are all scavengers.

Perhaps the best-known scavenger is the vulture. When an animal is sick or injured, vultures can often be seen circling overhead, waiting for it to die. When the animal is near death or dead, the vultures use their sharp beaks to dig into its hide.

A vulture has a bald head, which helps it to stay clean while it eats. Vultures have strong substances in their stomachs that stop them from getting ill from eating dead flesh. The largest vulture in the world is the Andean condor. It has a wingspan of up to 3.4 metres (11 feet)!

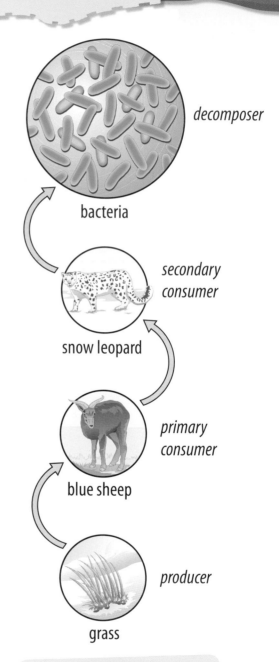

decomposer

bacteria

secondary consumer

snow leopard

primary consumer

blue sheep

producer

grass

Decomposers break down dead **organisms**.

This tiny snow flea is a decomposer that can survive harsh mountain conditions.

## Snow fleas

Tiny snow fleas can survive in harsh conditions, even where there does not seem to be any food. They live under the snow and come out to eat the remains of dead insects, **fungi**, and other waste that blow on to the tops of mountains.

Smaller decomposers include worms, maggots, and insects. They eat dead plants, animals, and animal waste. Dung beetles lay their eggs in other animals' droppings. When the eggs hatch, the beetle **larvae** feed on the droppings. This makes the droppings easier for **bacteria** to break down.

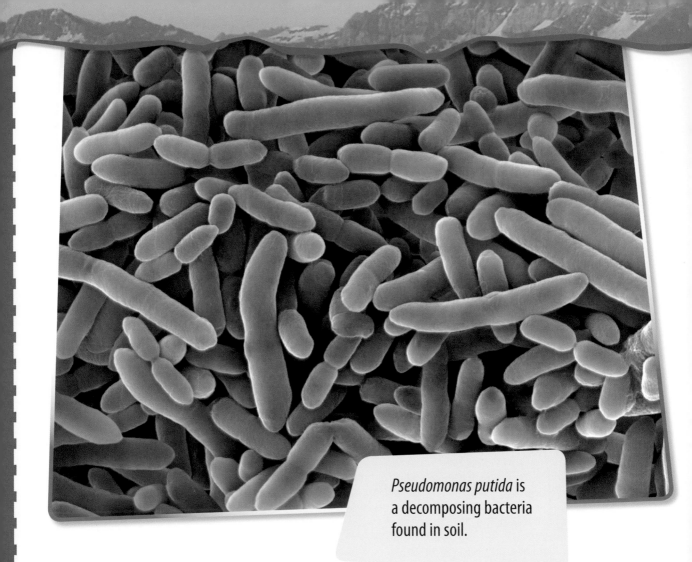

*Pseudomonas putida* is a decomposing bacteria found in soil.

## DECOMPOSERS

Decomposers break down dead plant and animal matter. They use some of the dead matter for **energy**. The rest breaks down into **nutrients** that end up in the soil. Plants need these nutrients to grow. Without decomposers there would not be any plants – or any food chains at all!

## BACTERIA

Millions of microscopic bacteria live in mountain soils. Many of these bacteria live in thin films of water that surround small particles of soil. Some of them feed on proteins and other chemicals in the bodies of other organisms. Others feed on the waste of other animals or even other bacteria.

## FUNGI

Fungi can often be seen clinging to tree trunks in the mountains or growing on fallen trees. Mushrooms, another kind of fungi, grow on the ground, especially in moist areas. Fungi have thin threads called hyphae that allow them to poke through large things like dead trees. Fungi use **enzymes** to break down plant and animal matter into nutrients. They use some of the nutrients themselves and release the rest into the soil.

### HUMONGOUS FUNGUS

An armillaria mushroom may look like a single organism. However, it is actually only a small part of a much larger organism. Underground, the mushrooms are connected by shoestring structures called rhizomorphs. This makes them a single organism. The largest armillaria is found in the Blue Mountains in Oregon in the US. Scientists believe it stretches over 965 hectares (2,384 acres). That makes it about as big as 1,665 football fields! It is the biggest organism on Earth. The armillaria is also very old. Scientists think it is about 2,400 years old.

These armillaria mushrooms are all connected by rhizomorphs.

# WHAT ARE MOUNTAIN FOOD CHAINS LIKE AROUND THE WORLD?

Mountain food chains are very different in different parts of the world. That is because different **species** are **native** to different parts of the world. Monkeys and snow leopards live on mountains in Asia, while grizzly bears make their home on mountains in North America. The **climate** also affects where animals live. Human activities have had a huge effect on food chains all around the world. People have changed food chains by clearing mountain forests and bringing in **non-native** species.

## LOSING A LINK: WATER SKINK

The Blue Mountains water skink is a lizard that lives only in the Blue Mountains in Australia. It eats mostly insects. Today, the water skink is **endangered**. People are destroying its habitat by building houses in the mountains. Many people who live in the mountains have house cats. The cats prey on the skinks, causing even more of them to die out.

The Blue Mountains water skink is an endangered species.

# THE ALPS

The Alps are a large mountain range that runs through several countries in Europe. These mountains cross Austria, Switzerland, Germany, France, Italy, and the Balkans. At 4,807 metres (15,770 feet), Mont Blanc is the tallest mountain in the Alps. Although the higher parts of the Alps are rocky with steep cliffs, many plants and animals have **adapted** to this **habitat**.

The chamois is a kind of goat that is well suited to steep, rocky cliffs. It has good balance and can jump 2 metres (6.5 feet) high. A chamois eats herbs and wildflowers in the warmer months and lichen, mosses, and pine shoots during the winter. A chamois may be eaten by a lynx. In addition to chamois, lynx eat smaller **prey** such as hares, foxes, rodents, and fish.

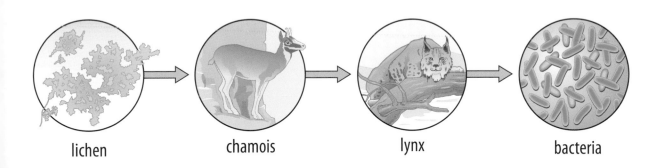

| lichen | chamois | lynx | bacteria |

This is an example of a food chain from the Alps mountain range.

# THE ANDES

The Andes in South America is the longest mountain range in the world. Rainforests in the lower **elevations** are home to thousands of different kinds of plant and animal. These forests are being cut down at rapid rates. Many species are now endangered.

One of these endangered species is the only bear native to Latin America. The Andean bear has an important role in the food chain. When it eats fruit, it swallows seeds that are too big for many other animals to eat. The seeds end up in the bear's waste. This helps spread new trees to different parts of the forest.

# EAST AFRICAN HIGHLANDS

The highest mountains in Africa are located in the East African highlands. This area is home to Mount Kilimanjaro and Mount Kenya. These mountains have rich **ecosystems** with many different kinds of plant and animal.

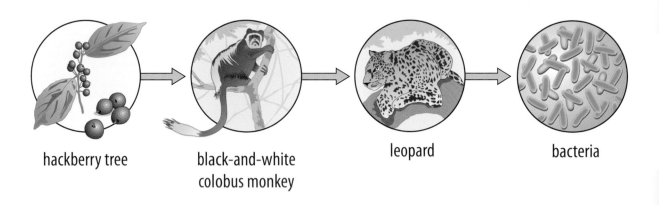

hackberry tree        black-and-white        leopard        bacteria
                      colobus monkey

This is a food chain
from Mount Kenya.

Rainforests thrive in the lower elevations. They provide food and homes for many animals. **Primary consumers** such as elephants, bongo antelopes, and colobus monkeys find trees, shrubs, berries, and grasses to eat in the rainforest. These animals must always be on the lookout for **predators**. A leopard hiding in the bushes might want to make a monkey its lunch.

## PROTECTING A LINK: BONGOS

By the 1960s, bongo antelopes on Mount Kenya were at risk. Illegal hunting and **deforestation** were killing off the animals. Zoos captured 30 bongos and took them to the United States. By the early 2000s, there were no bongos left on Mount Kenya. Zoos in the United States agreed to ship some of their bongos back to Africa. This gave the bongos a second chance in their natural habitat.

A female bongo antelope is seen here with her two cubs.

## THE ROCKY MOUNTAINS

The Rocky Mountains stretch nearly 5,000 kilometres (3,100 miles) from Alaska to Mexico. **Producers** in the Rockies include shrubs, grasses, and **conifers**. Pikas, marmots, snowshoe hares, moose, and other primary consumers depend on these plants for survival. These animals are eaten by **secondary consumers** such as bobcats, wolves, and golden eagles.

## THE HIMALAYAS

Fifteen of the world's tallest mountains, including Mount Everest, are in the Himalayas. The Himalayas are also home to some of the harshest habitats on Earth. Plants and animals that live here must be able to withstand violent storms, strong winds, freezing temperatures, and a lot of snow.

This food web shows how organisms are linked in the Rocky Mountains.

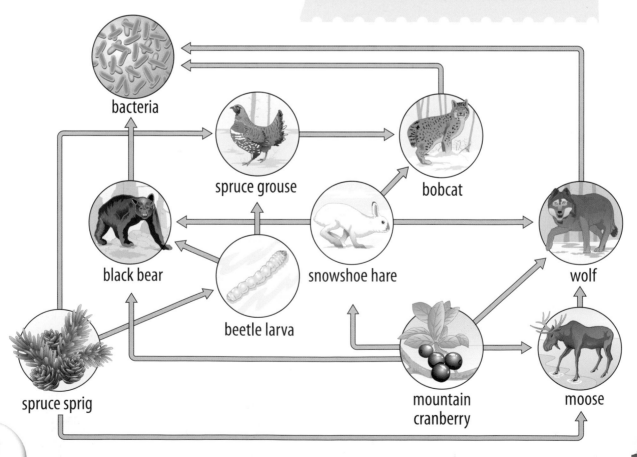

bacteria

spruce grouse

bobcat

black bear

snowshoe hare

wolf

beetle larva

mountain cranberry

moose

spruce sprig

This climate is hard on people as well as animals. Many people who live in the Himalayas have survived by raising **domesticated** animals such as sheep, goats, cows, and yaks. The animals **graze** in the high mountain meadows. Unfortunately, these animals are eating all the grass. There is not enough left for wild primary consumers such as marmots, ibex, musk deer, and wild yaks. With fewer primary consumers, secondary consumers cannot get enough to eat. People also cut down trees to use for building or for fuel. The loss of trees makes it harder for wild animals to find food and shelter.

## LOSING A LINK: PIKAS

**Global warming** is making life more difficult for pikas. Pikas are adapted to cold weather. Today's warmer weather is forcing them to move higher up in the mountains, where it is still cold. Scientists worry that the pikas will soon be able to survive only at the top of the mountain. Then they will run out of colder places to go.

This pika is gathering grass to line its burrow.

# HO' ' ARE HU. .ANS HAR. .ING MOUNTAIN FOOD CHAINS?

Food webs high up in mountain environments usually contain fewer links than those down below. That is because conditions are so harsh that only a few **species** can survive there. Food chains and webs in these places are less complex. Some species in these **habitats** are more at risk if something happens to their particular food source or habitat. Natural processes, such as earthquakes or avalanches, can further harm fragile mountain food chains. However, over the years, humans have damaged them much more.

Most animals cannot live in places where people have cut down all of the trees.

## HABITAT LOSS

When people move in, animals often have to move out. Human activity often harms, or even destroys, natural habitats. People cut down trees to use the wood for building and for fuel. People mine mountains for coal, oil, and minerals. They clear the land to build homes, plant crops, and **graze** animals.

The spotted owl in north-west North America is a victim of habitat loss. Logging companies have destroyed many forests where the owls live. When the owl became **endangered**, **conservation** groups were able to get laws passed to protect it. Now logging companies are no longer allowed to cut down trees near spotted owl habitats.

### BREAKING CHAINS: THE APPALACHIANS

For years, companies have mined for coal in the Appalachian Mountains. A process called **strip mining** often involves blowing the tops off mountains. This not only destroys the **ecosystem** but also creates a great deal of **debris**. The mining companies dump huge amounts of debris into the valleys, filling them in. The debris destroys mountain streams and habitats. Today, there are rocky grasslands where mountain forests once grew.

The mountain top has been removed at this coal mining site in the US.

## TOURISM IN THE MOUNTAINS

Many people enjoy visiting mountains. In fact, more people are choosing to travel to mountains than ever before. It would be great if people could spend time in mountain environments without affecting mountain food chains, but this is not possible. Tourists need roads, bridges, and tunnels for travelling. Once they get to where they are going, they need places to stay – campsites, cabins, lodges, and resorts. While they are in the mountains, people may hike, mountain bike, ski, hunt, or fish. All those roads, buildings, and people damage mountain habitats.

People do not always treat mountain habitats with respect. They often leave litter behind and **pollute** mountain streams and lakes. Hunters sometimes illegally kill animals out of season or in protected areas. People may accidentally start forest fires that can destroy huge areas of plants and animals. Even careful hikers may accidentally step on fragile mountain plants. Because of the short growing season at higher **elevations**, it takes longer for damaged plants to regrow.

Mountain climbers left this rubbish behind on Mount Everest.

Acid rain has killed this spruce forest.

## POLLUTION AND ACID RAIN

Burning **fossil fuels** causes **pollution**. People burn fossil fuels when they drive motor vehicles or burn wood or coal for fuel. Factories also burn a great deal of fossil fuel. When the fossil fuel mixes with rain water, it makes acid rain. Acid rain harms trees. It can destroy their leaves and, over time, kill them. It also damages mountain streams and lakes, killing the fish and other animals that live there.

### A BROKEN CHAIN: ADIRONDACK MOUNTAINS

Acid rain has had a terrible effect on the Adirondack Mountains in the US state of New York. Many streams, lakes, and ponds are so acidic that much of the plant and animal life has died. Some lakes no longer have any fish.

## CLIMATE CHANGE

Scientists believe that burning fossil fuels is causing temperatures to rise around the world. Warmer temperatures are not good for mountain habitats. When it gets too warm, animals **migrate** up the mountain in search of colder temperatures. They often end up in other animals' habitats, where they compete with them for food. Many mountain species will not be able to survive if temperatures rise too much.

Another effect of **climate change** is that it is causing winter snow to melt earlier in the spring and to melt faster. This will mean less water in the late summer for animals and for people. Many towns and cities get their drinking water from mountains. In addition, climate change results in drier conditions. This increases the danger of forest fires.

When snow melts too early in the spring, there is not enough water in late summer.

## A BROKEN CHAIN: TOO MANY PINE BEETLES

Pine beetles lay their eggs in the bark of lodge pole pine trees. When the eggs hatch, the **larvae** eat the tree from the inside out. This cuts off the tree's water supply. Soon the needles turn red, then grey. The beetles also carry a **fungus** that help it overcome the trees' defences and cause the tree to turn blue. Over time the tree dies. The pine beetle population used to be controlled by cold winter weather. Most of the beetles died when the temperature dropped. However, climate change has resulted in milder winters. Instead of dying, the beetles have multiplied at astounding rates. They have killed millions of trees in the northern United States and Canada. Other animals, such as squirrels and birds, depend on these trees for food and shelter. Large **grazers** such as caribou eat the lichen that grows under these trees. Without the lichen, the caribou may also disappear.

Pine beetles and their larvae kill the trees they live in.

# WHAT CAN YOU DO TO PROTECT MOUNTAIN FOOD CHAINS?

Food chains are not just for animals. People need them, too. Mountain trees create a great deal of the world's oxygen. They also stop the soil from **eroding**. This helps to prevent landslides, avalanches, and floods. People rely on water from mountain streams and rivers for growing crops, producing **hydroelectricity**, and drinking. In countries such as Peru and Tibet, people depend on the mountains for farming and **grazing** their animals. Mountain **habitats** are some of the most beautiful and amazing places in the world.

People are working to protect mountain habitats all over the world. Scientists study mountain **ecosystems** to learn how they are affected by human activities. Conservation groups work to help repair and protect mountains, too.

People will plant these pine saplings in an area where logging companies have cut down trees.

# REPAIRING HABITATS

There are many things people can do to help repair a damaged mountain habitat. Groups of people often work together to help a specific part of a mountain area. Picking up litter is a great way to help. Not only does litter look bad, it can harm animals that may think it is food and try to eat it. Planting **native** trees and shrubs is another good way to help. People can also keep trails clear so that walkers will not wander away from them and step on fragile native plants.

## A BROKEN CHAIN: NON-NATIVE PLANTS

Many mountain habitats have been taken over by invasive **non-native** plants. These plants crowd out native plants. Insects and other **primary consumers** can not eat these plants and are left without a food source. Clearing alien plants and planting native ones can make a big difference to the food web!

This park worker is spraying herbicide on a non-native **species** that was hurting native plants. But the **herbicide** can also harm the mountain habitat.

## PROTECTING HABITATS

Areas such as national parks and nature reserves are often protected by governments. Protected areas do allow some human activity. Most do not allow hunting, fishing, or the gathering of plants. Protected areas are also safe from building and mining. However, sometimes government protection is not strong enough, and species are put at risk.

Animals do not know where protected areas end. **Migrating** animals, such as elk, or animals with large territories, such as wolves, often end up on unprotected land. There they are in danger of being hunted. Some species are protected everywhere they go. Laws make it illegal to hunt **endangered** species.

This sign marks an area in which humans are trying to protect plants and animals native to the habitat.

HABITAT RESTORATION AREA

# TEACHING PEOPLE ABOUT FOOD CHAINS

**Conservation** groups teach people about fragile habitats. They teach them new ways to do things that do not damage mountain food chains. People in the Himalayas are learning to use kerosene instead of trees and brush for fuel. In the Andes, conservation workers are saving endangered **predators** by helping sheep herders protect their sheep. When herders know their sheep are safe, they do not need to protect them by killing lynxes, wolves, and bears.

These children are picking up litter in a stream that runs through a mountain range.

## *RESTORING THE CHILDREN'S FOREST*

Part of the US state of California's San Bernardino National Forest is known as the Children's Forest. It is home to a nature centre staffed by young volunteers. School groups, youth groups, and families come to the nature centre to learn about the forest. Children ages 11 to 17 also volunteer for all kinds of roles. They serve as hiking tour guides and wildfire lookouts.

In the Children's Forest Great Seeds Restoration Program, children help out by collecting seeds, growing seedlings, and planting trees. These replace trees destroyed by wildfires.

# TOP 10 THINGS YOU CAN DO TO PROTECT MOUNTAINS

There are many things you can do to protect mountain food chains. Here is a list of the top 10:

**1** Never drop litter when you are hiking in the mountains – or anywhere! Pack up your rubbish and leave campsites cleaner than when you arrived.

**2** Do not use chemicals such as washing-up liquid while you are camping. They can end up in mountain streams.

**3** Stay on marked trails so that you do not step on fragile mountain plants.

**4** Always stay on marked trails when hiking. This preserves plants and prevents the soil from **eroding**.

**5** Volunteer to plant trees in the mountains. Many **conservation** groups sponsor tree planting days. Or you could plant trees with your scout, guide, or youth group.

**6** Do not pick wildflowers or other **native** plants.

**7** To help prevent **climate change**, try to use less **fossil fuel**. Can you ride your bike or take a bus? How about sharing lifts to school and activities?

**8** Raise money for a conservation group. What can you do to earn money? Can you babysit, do gardening, or hold a cake sale?

**9** Write to your local councillor, or MP. Let them know why they should support laws that protect mountain **habitats**.

**10** Learn about food chains and tell other people about **endangered** plants and animals.

# GLOSSARY

**adapt** when a species undergoes changes that help it survive

**adaptation** special structures or behaviours that make an organism well suited to its environment

**alga** (plural **algae**) simple, plant-like organism

**alpine** relating to high areas of a mountain

**altitude** height above sea level

**bacterium** (plural **bacteria**) tiny living decomposer found everywhere

**carnivore** animal that eats only other animals

**clear-cutting** removal of all trees in an area

**climate** weather conditions in an area

**climate change** human-made changes in weather patterns

**conifer** kind of tree that produces seeds in a cone and has needle-like leaves that it does not lose in the autumn

**conservation** protecting and saving the natural environment

**consumer** organism that eats other organisms

**debris** pieces of broken rock or other waste

**decomposer** organism that breaks down and gets nutrients from dead plants and animals and their waste

**deforestation** cutting down or burning trees in a forest

**domesticated** trained or adapted to be of use to humans

**ecosystem** community of plants and animals and the area in which they live

**elevation** referring to a certain height

**endangered** at risk of dying out. Laws are in place to protect many endangered animals.

**energy** power needed to grow, move, and live

**enzyme** protein that speeds up a chemical reaction

**eroding** wearing away of rocks and soil by wind, water, ice, or chemicals

**fossil fuel** fuel that comes from the remains of plants and animals that lived millions of years ago

**fungus** (plural **fungi**) decomposer organism including mushrooms, toadstools, and their relatives

**global warming** worldwide increase in air and ocean temperature

**graze** eat grass and other green plants in a field or meadow

**grazer** large mammals that eat grasses. Sheep, cattle, zebras, and antelopes are grazers.

**habitat** place where an organism lives

**herbicide** chemical used to kill unwanted plants

# GLOSSARY

**herbivore** animal that eats only plants

**hibernate** rest for long periods to survive the winter

**hydroelectricity** electricity produced by the power of flowing water

**larvae** (singular: **larva**) young of some insects and other animals

**migrate** to move from one area to another

**mammal** warm-blooded animal that produces milk to feed its young

**native** plant or animal that lives in the place where it evolved

**nectar** sugary substance made by plants to attract pollinators

**non-native** plant or animal that lives in an area where it did not evolve

**nutrient** chemical that plants and animals need to live

**omnivore** animal that eats plants and other animals

**organism** living thing.

**photosynthesis** process that plants use to turn energy from the Sun into food and oxygen

**pollinate** fertilize a plant by transferring pollen from another plant

**pollinator** animal that carries pollen from the male part of a flower to the female part

**pollute** release harmful waste into the land, air, or water

**pollution** harmful waste

**predator** animal that hunts and eats other animals

**prey** animal that is eaten by another animal

**primary consumer** animal that eats plants

**primate** group of mammals that share certain features, such as hands that grasp and large brains for their body size

**producer** organism (plant) that can make its own food

**scavenger** organism that feeds on dead plants, animals, and their waste

**secondary consumer** animal that eats other animals

**species** type of plant or animal

**strip mining** method of removing coal or other minerals that completely strips away the soil

**summit** top of a mountain

**symbiosis** two organisms living together in a relationship that benefits both

**talon** claw of a bird of prey

**timberline** height on a mountain above which it is too cold and windy for trees to grow

# FIND OUT MORE

## BOOKS

*Extreme Habitats: Mountains*, Susie Hodge (Tick Tock Media, 2007)

*Geography Fact Files: Mountains,* Anna Claybourne (Hodder Wayland, 2007)

*Mapping Earthforms: Mountains*, Catherine Chambers and Nicholas Lapthorn (Heinemann Library, 2007)

*Wild Habitats of the British Isles*, Richard Spilsbury and Louise Spilsbury (Heinemann Library, 2005)

*World in Peril: Mountains Under Threat,* Paul Mason (Heinemann Library, 2010)

## WEBSITES

### www.mountain.org
The Mountain Institute's website offers more information about conserving mountains.

### http://kids.nationalgeographic.co.uk/Animals/CreatureFeature
The National Geographic website is packed with information about mountain animals, including videos, sound clips, and e-cards to send to your friends and family.

### http://www.mountaindays.net/mountains/index.php
Check out webcams and photos of UK mountains at the Mountain Days website.

### http://www.nationalparks.gov.uk/learningabout
Find out about National Parks and mountain conservation projects, and even plan a class field trip using this website.

### www.worldwildlife.org
The World Wildlife Fund works to protect nature and endangered species.

## FURTHER RESEARCH

Choose a topic from this book you'd like to research further. Do you live near a mountain you would like to know more about? Or is there a faraway mountain you think is exotic? Was there a creature in this book you find interesting? Is there something harming mountain food chains you'd like to know more about putting a stop to? Visit your local library to find out more information.

# INDEX